in Cars

Also by Kimmy Beach

Nice Day for Murder: Poems for James Cagney
Alarum Within: Theatre Poems
fake Paul

in Cars

Kimmy Beach

TURNSTONE PRESS

Turnstone Press
Artspace Building
018-100 Arthur Street
Winnipeg, MB
R3B 1H3 Canada
www.TurnstonePress.com

Turnstone Press gratefully acknowledges the assistance of the Canada Council for the Arts, the Manitoba Arts Council, the Government of Canada through the Book Publishing Industry Development Program, and the Government of Manitoba through the Department of Culture, Heritage and Tourism, Arts Branch, for our publishing activities.

Cover design: Doowah Design
Interior design: Sharon Caseburg
Printed and bound in Canada by Friesens for Turnstone Press.

Library and Archives Canada Cataloguing in Publication

Beach, Kimmy, 1964-
In cars / Kimmy Beach.

Poems.
ISBN 978-0-88801-325-5

1. Rural youth—Canada, Western—Poetry. 2. Automobiles—Poetry.
I. Title.

PS8553.E119I5 2007 C811'.6 C2007-901879-3

for Dawn Andrea Beach
1978–1998

and

for D. J. W.
1964–1980

Contents

in Cars

I.

There's a voice in my head that drives my heel

—"Radar Love"

Roller Boogie

[Wheelies Roller Rink, 1982]

I park *Fernando*   my '67 Ford
Falcon station wagon (black where it's not rusted)
next to Susan's Nova
the lot full of muscle cars and beaters
idling   revving   teenagers smoking   drinking beer
the green Demon is Joseph's new ride
he calls it *Chick Magnet*
Keith's yellow Challenger is the sexiest car here
since he's put the Rallyes on it he can peel out better
all steaming leather and total Mopar Muscle

I walk past the lineup at the door
skates tossed over my shoulder
call *Hi Terry!* over everyone's heads
he buzzes me in through the lobby doors
I don't have to pay   I work here

> I used to work concession
> everybody starts back there up to their necks
> in spilled pop syrup   slipping in butter
> an oily-fingered slickness you can't quite wash away
> rancid yellow giving away how you make your money
> or worse, behind the skate counter
> spraying sweaty rentals with that deodorant shit
> skating in rentals is like wearing
> tape on your glasses
> the fuzziest boot covers in the world can't hide
> dirty orange rental wheels
> the feel of other people's sweat moving into your socks
>
> I like to dry-mop after the skaters have left
> collect the dirt of the evening   a shake
> out the side door into a dark lot

sometimes Terry will let me change the record
and now that I'm eighteen my favourite job is
Skate Cop   I have a whistle I blow when someone cuts
across the rink or speed skates on kids' night
start going the wrong direction just to be an
asshole you get whistled

tonight I'm here to skate
my hair is curled in a White Shoulders cloud I sprayed over my head
stepped, eyes closed, into the falling mist
my KC and the Sunshine Band concert T-shirt
tight across my breasts
Susan has seen me and waves from the rink
Joseph and Keith play foosball near the rental booth
Keith's Rock and Roll mullet swings around his face
when he flips the handles on the game
Joseph's moves tight and controlled
a small gold cross dangles just below his throat
blond hair styled and smooth

Terry spins "Celebration" by Kool & the Gang
kids in orange booths along the edge of the rink
sip Coke through straws
eat two-day-old popcorn
wrinkled wieners
Terry glides from the office
whistle on a chain around his neck
he's two feet taller than me
skates on and me still in my runners

What do you want for slow skate? he asks
"Cool Change" by Little River Band
and the Eagles' "I Can't Tell You Why"
Terry and I have been listening to those songs since grade 11
he kisses the top of my head   *You got it*

on the rink
a parade of Jordache Hi-Cut bell bottoms
head after head of waving
feathered hair   home perms
blonde highlights   blue sparkle eye shadow
a whiff of Youth Dew from frosted hair
polyester and shoulder pads
long chains on the boys   AC/DC T-shirts
our nightly ceremonies of armour and scent

I throw my Converses and denim jacket into a locker
pin the key to the back pocket of my brand-new Fancy Ass jeans
carry my skates to a red-carpeted bench
the breeze from my friends' revolutions
stirs my hair at the rinkside
a race to no place at the Speed of Disco

I glide to the can
my jeans are too new but otherwise
I'm looking good
my hair is straight at the back   feathered sides
put on some Chocolate Lip Smackers
tuck the tube into my front pocket

my skates are white Sure-Grip high-top Century Super X5L
with precision bearing wheels, split leather linings, adjustable
trucks, and axles that won't lose it cranked wide open
I keep my toe stops tight, axles oiled,
trucks loose for better cornering

first thing I did was replace the factory Sure-Grips
with top-of-the-line All American Dreams
the hottest wheels for 1982
they're worth the extra bucks for the looks I get from the guys
envious glares from girls
lots of them have All American Plus
they're an okay wheel but
a step down
Dreams give you smooth ride and speed

no boot covers for me
I like the beat-up look of my skates
black grooves the laces have made
in the leather   scuffs and creases show I'm serious
not afraid to enter the speed skate contest
or dance with Chris, the best waltzer at the rink
these skates have propelled me across paved school lots
kicked the sides of cars and buildings
carried me to friends and boys
held me up on eight white wheels

I wait for Susan to come around
take two spins with her while I look for Joseph
the floor worn under our wheels

when the rink was new, we could see
ourselves reflected in its surface
now it's an upside-down sheet of scratched sky
scuffed and loved
the disco ball spinning under a bank of speakers at the centre

Katie is crying in the back corner again
her best friend Barb holds her shoulders
Joseph's an asshole, Katie
you should break up with him
she won't do it
they've been having the same conversation
every night for three weeks

Joseph is at the DJ booth
he's been outside for a du Maurier
when I ride up next to him, he smells of smokes and cool rain
Terry puts on "Rapture" by Blondie
I spin backwards, catch Joseph's eye
tilt my head at him
he takes the step down from the carpeted booth
and catches up to me
we dance to the cool sounds
chat about his new skate wheels   Joseph guides me
around slow skaters   touching the hip
of my jeans to shift me over

When I Skate

you need a great song like "Urgent" by Foreigner
or "Bang a Gong" by T-Rex
just the right pace and beat
I'm the best skater girl on the rink Friday nights
lots of other girls have more makeup
more expensive jeans
but nobody beats my moves
my killer skates and beat-up wheels

my calves are firm and lean
friendship bracelets ride my wrist
under the cuffs of my white blouse

my skates fly me through the building
coloured lights on my hair and shoulders
I rex along the straightaways
scrape the edges of my wheels every few seconds
to slow myself down behind slower skaters
or just show off my noisy skates

I take the next corner   my right skate points forward
the left faces backward
I lean into the curve, legs spread, my body's momentum
carries me through the turn
my skates in opposite directions

I build up speed on the long path to the next corner
hold myself tall and coast fast
add a tiny push to the side if I start to slow
my trucks always oiled   sail the length of the rink
body straight   arms at my sides
letting bass guitars pulse through my wheels

up my legs   into my groin
I'm strong and turned on
my jeans tug at me   I lean back into a curve at the corner
pull one foot back behind the other
let it hit the rink hard
in a reverse crossover along the straight edge

I close my eyes for just a second longer than it's safe
feel the air on my eyelids   at my throat
Susan will join me halfway through the song
we rex side by side   our skates in perfect rhythm
crossing over on the same beat
the right skate lifts from the floor before each crossover
left then right on the long stretches of rink

she skates behind me
holds the belt loop at the back of my jeans
we are a gorgeous train of perfume
hair spray   perfect synchronicity
we're irresistible and we skate
effortlessly
our pulses listen and match the music
hair bobbing at our temples in response to the movement
her fingers at my spine
skates carrying us

Double Action Trucks

I love to watch him take the corners
push through the turns   his GWGs
stretched over his legs

> Joseph's roller skates are souped-up hot rods
> Riedell 220 boots with full-lined leather uppers and soles
> Snyder Deluxe plates and Double Action trucks
> he's replaced the factory suspension with the professional
> Sure-Grip upgrade kit and uses the truck tension tool
> to deal with slight differences in flexibility
> from Sure-Grip trucks to Snyder body
> his white Star HD75 wheels (the high-end industry standard
> for indoor dance and rink) were a luxury purchase

with Katie he's smooth and sure on the rink
his bright white wheels lift and turn, touch on blue
blond hair   thick brows
tight yellow T-shirt tucked into worn jeans

I lean at the edge of the DJ booth
pretend I'm not watching them
pretend to listen to Terry   he's showing me
John Lennon's last album   the one he made just before
he got shot in the head   rain mixing with blood on a
cool December New York street
Joseph's hands on Katie's waist   they waltz close
she skates backwards
they make their own breeze and her hair
swirls around her face
her forearms easy on his shoulders
hands dangling above his back
his dirty blond hair touching her wrist

Bush Party

I've been friends with Terry since Osland's French 9 class
Terry and I fucked for a while but I'm over it
we're easy friends
everybody fucks everybody else around here
you just don't advertise

I sit in the centre of the front seat next to him
couple of pals driving home   that's all
his right arm around my shoulders
I lean into him the way you're supposed to tuck yourself
against the boy driving you home
we've drifted and just miss the truck in the other lane
horn fading into a lower note past us
            I scream   turn Terry's face to look
at the road not at me
he pulls his right hand from behind my head
reaches for the wheel
he's been confessing   *I still love you*
says he has since that grade 10 *Macbeth* scene we did
for Gibson's English class
Was the hope drunk wherein you dressed yourself?
he's calm though we've nearly just
died

I catch my breath
            we're drunk
and I think
about Joseph

Terry brought Strawberry Angel for me to drink at the party
bushes filled with teenagers
classmates I barely know
I never hang out with the jocks and heads at school
unsure without my skates   without the disco
and new wave of my blue-floored rolling kingdom
Terry's the only friend I have here
my other friends   smarter than me   gone skating

the heads throw gasoline and half-empty vodka bottles
on the bonfire to make it rage into the night sky
"Keep It Comin' Love" pounds
distorted from someone's Camaro   its trunk open and
music spilling
fragmented and screechy from brown panel speakers
pulled out of the wide-open car
aimed at the centre of the party
headlights from four or five muscle cars   couple of pickups
around the fire shining on one another across the smoke
a tightening circle of metal and tungsten
logs, glass, licks of flame

couples move off into firelit half-darkness
sweatshirts and jeans and blue Bisons
football jackets in various stages of struggle
shaken from impatient boy-arms
jackets and blankets already under the legs and bare
backs of girls I sat behind in Physics
Terry and I sit near the fire
brush sparks from sneakers   each other's sleeves

my plastic glass is full of strawberry wine
warm with bugs and ashes
from the fire floating   it tastes wonderful
sweet and right   and Terry's hand on my back

I think Terry's okay
to drive but I don't know
the yellow centre line a broken snake under us   beside us
another five K to my turnoff
clunkclunk of crisscrossed lines of tar like
bodies across the road

shut my eyes a second
see us   from above
a weaving black '67 Dart 170 V8 Convertible
on bare straight secondary highway
headlights two blind swerving eyes bleary
on the invisible road ahead

last year in bumper cars at Klondike Days
crashing for fun   Terry and I howled and
whooped   our necks
shocked from side to side at impact
hands slipping in other people's sweat
seats sticky from the teenagers who crashed ahead of us

Terry aimed laughing for me again and again
till long after I wasn't having fun anymore
jolts through my spine   elbows hyperextended
to keep the shock from my shoulders and spine
and strangers pummelled me from each side
jolted from behind   Terry's low-throated *Woo Hoo!*

Terry watches the road   tries to drive
straight as he can in a blind car
what the hell am I doing out here?
almost dying with another guy

Terry pulls me to him when we get to my place
kisses me   *I want you back*
beer smell stale and hard on his mouth
mom left the porch light on
the light between me and home
legs shaky as I climb out of the Dart

Fernando

fuzzy dice (two sets   one orange, one black)
peanut butter jar for gas money
Fernando is hideous to look at (he's a station wagon for godsakes)
but he can *go*
he's got a 351 Windsor 2-Barrel automatic
with power steering *and* power brakes
and a magic tailgate   it opens down or swings out

paid a buck for it on my sixteenth birthday
I changed the plugs, oil filter, and thermostat
rebuilt the carb and the radiator with Terry's help

the car's got a crappy sound system
just an AM push button radio but I can crank it
The Knack! I love this song!
"M-m-m-my Sharona"!

rusted metal   jagged edges under black carpet floor mats
when you lift the passenger side mat
you can see everything zinging by underneath

Windshield Ride

leaving the rink, Susan and I call
goodnights *fuck you*s across
high revs cranked radios
Keith yells *Hey babes! Let me give you a ride to your car*
it's ten yards away but what the hell?

we climb in behind the passenger seat
Chris crawls onto the hood hangs on
to windshield wipers
stoned midnight joy ride
on the hood of Keith's Challenger
one leg bent up for grip against the sloped metal hood
feels like a hundred miles an hour
Keith squealing the wheel
rubber stench in snow
Susan and me yelling for him to fucking stop

the car could shake Chris off a wiper
gnarled back snapped off
in his hand the car a pissed-off rodeo bull
bucking him off arms
swirling around his head tossed in front of wheels
Keith unable to stop even slow down

thunk thunkthunk
brake pedal screeched to the floor
a crushed head blood forced
from thighs, lungs

they make another pass   spitting pebbles and sand
Keith slows   Chris jumps off the hood
Fuck, man!   they slap palms
we climb out shaken and pale   run from the car
Chris climbs into the passenger seat
Keith's tires already smoking
rubber kissing pavement

Tonite Is a Wonderful Time to Fall

after the rink, we lie on Susan's bed among the jungle
stuffed animals   Raggedy Ann dolls
froofy pillows sewn by her grandmother
Susan thinks it's morbid to keep those but her mom
would kill her if she got rid of the cross-stitched bear cubs
faded purple tassels that totally clash with her bedroom

at least her mom let her pick the colours
her walls are bright yellow   a huge Leif Garrett poster
smiles down on us from the ceiling
he's dressed in his black shimmery suit from the cover
of *Feel the Need*   hands on his slim hips   tight red tank top
blond feathered mullet and big sincere teeth
he was pretty cute when we were sixteen
Susan either too nostalgic or lazy to climb up there
relegate him, rolled up, to her closet with Andy Gibb

Leif hangs there sagging
slightly at the waist from two years stuck to the ceiling
watching her nighttime explorations of herself
or some roller boy when her mom
and dad go away for the weekend

What am I gonna do, Soos? I really like Joseph
I don't think he's going around with Katie anymore

Susan throws both feet in the air for leverage
pendulums herself to a standing position
replaces the needle on the record player
to the beginning of "Tonite Is a Wonderful Time
to Fall in Love" by April Wine

it's the thirteenth playing
we pledge twenty times before we'll take it off
replace it with David Soul's "Don't Give Up On Us, Baby"

Susan says   *Joseph needs some help noticing*
What do you want?
landing back on the bed and shaking
the menagerie

I want Joseph

You've got to make him jealous then
He's gotta think you're going around with somebody else
What about Keith? You just said
he's still got the hots for you
          (her hand goes to her forehead)
Oh god! I love that key change

I love it too
Keith is a good target   he's buddies with Joseph
sure to tell him whatever goes on between us
I'll ask him to the drive-in   just as friends
we're silent while April Wine
rides us over and over into the night

April Wine is right
tonite *is* a wonderful time to fall
into something   if not love

For Your Eyes Only

Keith picks me up in his Challenger at eight
holds the passenger door   makes sure I buckle up
mom stands arms crossed on the porch
holding the screen door open with her hip
he waves as we drive off
honks his horn twice   she doesn't wave back

Listen to my new speakers
out of mom's earshot, he cranks the stereo
"Highway to Hell" pumps from the back seat
the distortion rattles my head
the air in the car boozy and close

we drive to The Stardust Drive-In at the edge of the city
park near the back

the movie is *For Your Eyes Only*
I'm dying to see it
Roger Moore (way too old) as Bond. James Bond.
        I like Connery better   the thick lisp
        the single-malt accent

Keith has stashed a six-pack under the passenger seat
        I don't like beer but I'll have one tonight
he cracks us one each
we clink the cans together
Just friends, right?   I ask him
he takes a long swig   *Just friends   No offence*
but you know I like Susan
puts his beer on the dash
hooks the speaker over the glass

after the Pink Panther cartoon
Bond through the gun barrel   he fires his Walther PPK
blood curtain oozes down the screen   I sip my beer

I've looked forward to this moment, Mr. Bond
Blofeld says to James, who's trapped in the helicopter
there's this ATAC code machine
that can make submarines fire on British targets
James Bond's mission is to find and disarm it

as 007 dumps Blofeld down a smokestack
and the opening credits begin
Keith finishes his beer and tosses the can into the back seat
reaches under my seat with his left hand
leans over me, brushes his cheek
against my breasts
his hair smells clean   sweet
he stops, beer in hand, kisses my collarbone
then my mouth
I tell him to cut it out   *I want to watch the movie*

he leans back hard   *Fuck!*
opens the can   downs it fast
my cheeks are hot   shoulders tense

a naked Sheena Easton sings the theme song
more naked women swim in languid underwater
silhouette   Bond in firing stance
I love BondMovie credits but tonight I can't pay attention
Keith hitting
the steering wheel with his palms

he's going to lean over me again
I reach under my seat to grab him
another beer before he can
    I don't know whether he's safer drunk or sober
    I don't know him at all
he takes it   opens it   it's gone
he throws the can to the floor
my beer is on the dash   he says *You gonna drink that?*
I shake my head and he reaches for it
my eyes never leaving the screen
I push flat back into the seat as his arm
stretches across me

Keith drinks the fourth beer more slowly
a few car doors slam during the blabby scene after the credits
guys going for popcorn and Cokes
he says *I gotta take a piss*
in the rear-view mirror I watch him weave to the can
I dig in my purse   mom put a Mad Money twenty in before I left
James makes his escape in the Bond Girl's yellow Citroen
not a true Bond getaway car but the Lotus
Q rigged for him back at headquarters has already blown up

   maybe Keith got lost   couldn't remember where he parked
   if I get out now I could be at the phone before he gets back
   my door is stuck   I'm hurting my shoulder
   I remember it's locked

the driver's door opens   Keith gets in heavy-
lidded and drunk
he reaches for more beer
this time he puts it on the dashboard unopened

one hand to the back of my head
forcing his tongue into me
the other hand between my legs
hard   *I want to watch the movie*

he pulls back
You asked me here to watch a fuckin movie?
his hands are at my blouse
the fabric tears from the buttons
I push him from my neck
the handle lets me go and I fall out of the car
my palms scrape on gravel
leave him panting halfway into the passenger seat
empty beer cans on the floor
I snatch my purse from the seat
run to the concession   one hand holding my blouse

a crying girl is on the phone   I turn back to the screen
there's a blonde teenage figure skater
in James' bed when he comes back to his hotel room
he pulls back slightly
resisting her advances without appearing rude
she looks disappointed but kisses him anyway

~

I don't know how the movie ends, though I'm sure
the ATAC is recovered from the underwater wreckage and Bond
gets the girl
her breathless *Oh James* in his ear
his mouth on hers
tender   not forceful
but enough to silence her into giving in

I Ran

the cab drops me off at the rink
let myself in and flick on a few lights
power to the turntables
dig through 45s till I find A Flock of Seagulls

"And I Ran"

skate off Keith's hands
his boozy breath on my neck
What the fuck was I thinking?   *Nothing is worth this*

in the half light, I skate and skate
hard till I roll off the memory
of him touching me   all that
hair   his brutal grip   cologne and sweat   that mouthwatering car
I screech to a halt each end of the rink
my wheels scraping on blue
let my skates slam the wall

~
mom sits curled up at the left side
of the old brown sofa
watching *Dynasty*
there's a cigarette in her right hand
she saw the cab
Did you and your friend have fun?

Next Day at the Rink

Keith pulls up beside me
floors the gas pedal a couple of times
Nazareth grinds from the speakers
"Love Hurts"
he gets out of the car presses his groin
against my driver's window
I give him the finger
bash his crotch with the door
that makes him move
grab my skates from the floor
everything's totally normal

he traps me against my car his thigh between mine
his hand bends my waist toward him
You're not seriously mad, are you?
I don't want to talk to him
I look away
he moves his face with mine
hair touching my shoulder
he's sniffing me

Hey, how about trying me out? Everyone
thinks we're screwing anyway
he holds my cheek

You wish I shoot back
slap his hand away and laugh
brush his arm as I move past him across the parking lot
"Ballroom Blitz" pounds from the rink
when Katie and Barb come outside for a smoke

Barb and I avoid eye contact
Katie whispers   *slag*
as my hand reaches the handle
but I know she wants Keith   she can have him
Keith behind me
one hand holding the door for me
the other on my shoulder

I cut across the rink
to the safety of Susan and Terry

Red Impala Convertible

fast lane on Highway 16, two guys next to us
in a red Impala Convertible with white
pace-car stripes down the hood
they pull up on Susan's side
matching the speed of my station wagon
in a seesaw forward and back

they open a window
Susan rolls hers down   puts her hands
over her hair so she won't lose careful curls in the wind

Where you headed, baby? he screams through highway noise
he hugs the centre line
close as he can get without hitting me

Susan leans back so I can talk to the guy
I recognize them from skating
rental boys but not bad-looking

Rink!
Okay, see you there!

the Impala roars off ahead
driver tugs sharp on the wheel
the tail end swings in front of us
kicks up snow and salt
scrapes and paws the bare patches
I pull over to the slow lane   let the car
show off on the ice

its left side faces us   screeches
down the highway passenger doors first
driver's window lifts
underside of the Chevy whirls ahead of us
lifts itself, tilting, off the road
it rolls over the highway   baseball hats fall from heads
the Impala spirals into the ditch   spins twice in the air
crazy juggling of tires and snow
hood crushed and the whine of a broken axle
tires hit again in the field
my feet hard on the brake pedal
arms hyperextended   hands white
on the wheel   tires squealing through my chest

two boys fly through glass
thump in heaps in the soft snow
the driver's side wheels lift again
a last half-revolution
before the car crash-lands on its roof
wheels turning free in air

pull over as far as I can   stop on the shoulder
I can't breathe
boys lie in blood on snow
legs twisted   heads still

all the doors swing open
exhaust pours from both cars
bloodied faces
an Impala wheezes its last

I drop to my knees   vomit between my frozen fingers
Susan screams into her mittens

Fat Windshield Gashes

I'm too shaky to drive
call Terry   he picks me up in his convertible
what the hell would I do without Terry?
I climb in at the police station
        (get me the fuck out of here! been here all afternoon
    answering questions about
    Were you dragging?
    Did you know those boys?
    How did the rollover happen?

        one of them died
    I told the cop I'd maybe seen them around the rink
    but I didn't know them   they were rentals   I never skate
    with rental boys
    and anyway they were the ones dragging not me
    like you can drag in a '67 Falcon 2-Barrel station wagon
    that's what I said   *Did you SEE my car? I wasn't racing*
    They were way ahead of me showing off
                                I stopped and we tried to help
                                We put our coats on them

    couple of kids in a crappy car, I guess
    must be out to fuck something up)

Terry spins us all over the big nine-to-five parking lots
the empty industrial area next to the rink
yellow striped spots   a place to trap the cars of
lawyers and secretaries and crabby women
in medical labs

we screech through the slush
stinking rubber
I take my seat belt off   stand on my seat
and Terry tailspins for me
his right arm around my legs inside the car
holding me steady

his foot heavy hitting
every one of his two hundred
and seventy-five horses
as high and hard as they can ride
it's fucking freezing and I don't care
Terry's left hand anticipates
direction of skid on ice
maximum swing on the back end sends me
reeling against the windshield laughing
tears freeze as soon as they leave my eyes
my hands up   wind sinking into me
I'd like to freeze like this forever
never move   never drive again
my hips part of the car
metal edge of the open roof pawing me
and I'm so alive

Stupid Impala Boy

that stupid show-off Impala boy should be
cruising still
buying some real skates
trying to pick up roller chicks like me at the rink

instead he's a dead body twisted and unmoving
fat windshield gashes on the sides of his head
because of me

Fancy Ass

we lie on our backs on Susan's bed
run the clothes hanger hook
through the hole in the zipper tabs and tug
our Fancy Ass jeans over our hips
they've been in the dryer on Extra Hot
for the past two hours

our big curling irons plugged in
side by side in the bathroom
two matching weapons
we pull long hair through gunmetal tongs
twirling it back to feather at our ears
a good shot of Final Net spray
sizzles on the metal

blue sparkle eye shadow, white blouses
White Shoulders misted over wrists and hair
tiny pearls at the hollows in our throats

it's Friday night Adult Skate, nine to twelve
I park *Fernando* next to Keith's Challenger
there's Terry's convertible
Joseph's '71 Demon next to it
we swish past the smokers, moms and kids
just coming out of Family Skate
Susan and I don't *do* family skate
too many stumbling brats
(their arms waving crazy
clacky little orange wheels
kicking out   falling in front of us)
not enough guys there to notice our hair
our tight little asses

tonight my extra loose trucks give just the right air
of casual disregard for the skates, though they're worth more
than my car
we hit the blue floor
Keith skates up behind Susan
his hands low at her waist   his eyes on me
Heard about that Impala crash, he says
Those boys too busy looking at your tits to watch the road?
Susan slaps him away, grabs my hand
Fuck off, Keith
we cut across the rink to the far side
against the rules
Terry won't whistle us

Keith steps off onto the carpet   his eyes
bright in the disco lights
she ignores him each time around the rink
his eyes lidded   he's just pissed Susan told him to get lost
after the drive-in thing

I gotta go to the can
Susan spins backwards, lands on her toe stops
hits the carpet   smooth past the DJ booth
she's gone ten minutes   misses "Stayin' Alive"
finally joins me, her blouse untucked
face a stone   hand freezing
when she takes mine

she skates ahead to avoid the idiot
slow couple who won't move to the inside

whispers to me that Keith pulled her outside
he's sick of the flirting and told her
do it with him or he'd tell everyone what a
virgin she is
how she and I tried to make him look like an asshole
with that drive-in trick
couple of cockteases

I see a flash of angry skin through
her jeans ripped where Keith
cut her with his pocket knife when she tried to skate
away from him   gravel   snow   pavement
slowing her down

she doesn't want to talk about it
skates ahead
her wheels leave a faint melted
trail on the floor
wet fear and wounded flesh

Joseph and Katie Dance on a Saturday Night for the Last Time

this skate is *for old time's sake*, I guess
Katie wants to go around with Keith
be seen in his Challenger
she wants to get felt up at the drive-in
wants Keith's long blond hair swaying at her nipples
she knows he'll fuck her

tonight Joseph finally asks me
if I want to go for coffee   a real date
at Last Skate I move to a bench
undo laces   tie them together
steps unsteady without wheels under me
heart unsteady as Joseph waits at the exit

he says he'll bring me back to my car later
holds his passenger door open for me
I toss my skates into the back seat
my wheels clink against his
I love his car   bright green
with black stripes on the sides
I watch him slide into the driver's seat
the interior is black leather
he always smells of it when he comes into the rink
cool and sure
               I'm nervous about what to say
he revs it too high
noise and exhaust   he peels out
Katie watches us from the lobby

I watch Joseph's hands on the wheel
feel the seat's cool black under my thighs
spread my legs a little to feel
the pound of bass through leather
"Turn Me Loose" by Loverboy
the music's too loud to talk about anything

I don't drink coffee but tonight
at Shakey's Pizza I drink three cups
Joseph talks about his new car
The disc-brake swap was the first change I made
My Demon's were nearly shot
I had some A-Body spindles from my dad's old '74 Swinger
so I dropped those in
he's replaced the exhaust tips
upgraded the drive train and rechromed the mirrors
leather seats in the back all shined up

I tell him about the carb I rebuilt
and he says he thinks
he really likes me
I told Keith keep away from you or I'll beat the crap out of him
he studies his coffee cup
Do you want to go around with me?

Yes

we pull up to my station wagon in the rink's parking lot
I take my skates from the Demon
throw them over my shoulder
lean against my passenger door embarrassed
my ugly car!   my right skate clunks the window behind me

he leans against me, winces and pulls back
I shift the other skate out of his ribs
we laugh   nervous
skates clatter to pavement

his mouth on mine is sweet
coffee flavoured
I feel stiffness in his jeans
my own thigh under his
fingers against his leg
my car pushing me closer to him
his hands moving to my breasts
my hand between us now
at his chest
later
later

Friday Night Waltz Contest

the music is KC and the Sunshine Band
"Please Don't Go"
the wrong tempo for true waltzing
I could make it work
Terry's the judge tonight
I'm a cinch to win no matter who I dance with
first prize is the *For Your Eyes Only* soundtrack
even after what happened at the drive-in, I want that record
Sheena Easton is totally cool on it

Joseph finds me at the DJ booth
Will you dance this one with me?
I hold out my hand
let him lead me onto the rink
he skates backwards, my two hands in his, my skates
moving on their own
his momentum pulls me to the centre
he takes me in his hands and we begin the dance
like we've always known the moves
each other's bodies
click of my wheels on plastic
lazy lift and drop
the skates part of my body
Joseph's hands carrying me
we whirl past other couples
figure eight around Keith and Katie at the centre
trust Joseph to steer me clear of curved brick walls
our wheels leave the floor   click down again
we add a touch of face-to-face disco rexing
when the bass line gets heavier
he holds my waist in his right hand

my right hand in his left   we fly around the corner
me spinning backwards to take the edge
my grasp on his hand tighter for balance
skates turn me and I see us
lifting from the rink   moving high over other
dancers   spin of the record on the turntable
an upward river of notes from the faraway
needle   our wheels turning free in air

he guides me into the next corner
sides of my wheels scraping the floor
to control my speed and direction
bending of leather boots
I raise my heels from the floor
spin twice on my front wheels
under the loose grip of his fingers

I settle back into his arms   the length of his body
my breasts against his chest
our skates manoeuvring around one another
he spins to face me   I guide him around the other dancers
he keeps his eyes on me
sings to me in a quiet voice
Please don't go

he pulls me to him as I come out of spins
tightens his fingers above my back pocket
holds me steady   doesn't take his eyes from my mouth
my eyes   his lips in a half smile, singing
my hand at the edge of his collar
warmth of dirty blond hair
the cool clasp of his gold chain under my fingertips

we pull out of our embrace near the end of the song
skate side by side for one more circle of the rink
holding hands in a slow rex
we cut to the centre, our skate wheels screech
in a perfect side stop and he hugs me
I inhale his trace of sweat and cologne
his hands on my ass now
moving up my back
his long thighs   breath in my ear

we pull apart   wait for Terry's decision
he slips from the booth
All American Dreams spinning at his heel
stops inches from me
hands me the new album
Terry turns, wordless
skates back to change the record

Joseph gives me a quick kiss on the cheek
We were great, honey

I whisper back
Meet me here at two in the morning
my feathered hair sways behind me as I skate past Terry to the can
check my lipstick, the fit of my jeans
hands buzzing
my throat on fire

My Skates in a Tangle on the Rink

five keys on the ring I toss
into the air and catch   once   twice
I'll be in deep shit if we get caught in here this late

Joseph squeals his Demon into the parking lot
pulls up in front of me
the car roaring   revving
David Bowie pouring out the open windows
he pumps the brakes to make the car
lurch   forward   in spurts
the green beast sniffs the air   eager to ride
he leans out the window
You got your keys? he yells over "Rebel Rebel"
the car vibrating around him
I lean on the damp brick of the two-in-the-morning rink
wait for him to hurry up and park his car

I open the front door   Joseph behind me
open the inner door   the office
shut off the alarm
flip the breakers to turn on the disco ball
power to the turntables
Joseph follows me everywhere
peel his hands from my breasts
tease my throat from his mouth

I toss him the keys for the record case in the DJ booth
he pulls out
Pink Floyd, Black Sabbath
puts them aside
he knows I want Blondie   Depeche Mode
Gary Numan

I lace up my skates   their tongues still supple
from the Friday night skate that ended two hours ago

the turntable crackles
"Heart of Glass"
Joseph throws his skates on
stuffs the laces into the tops
he hits the rink
slides to where I wrap laces once
around the tops of my boots
        he lifts me
        we loop and kiss
his jeans tight   blue of his denim jacket
scratchy and warm under my wrists

he guides me to the floor under the speakers
pretends to trip me   he knows I'm too sure-footed
to fall for it
but I decide to fall
my blouse gives way to his fingers
he's hard against me   grinding me against the rink
I open to him   let him kiss one exposed tit
pull him to me by his ass
his wheels clunk the floor
the rink is cool through my jeans
his cock hot and in rhythm
with Blondie's churning bass line

I stop him, breathless
Go put on KC and the Sunshine Band
he skates to the booth and digs out "Please Don't Go"
I kick off my skates and jeans and lie back
naked from the waist at the centre of the floor
green and red lights curve across my body
he kneels over me
scoops me up at the waist
his eyes grey-blue and shining
he takes my mouth
his cheeks are rough   his tongue on mine

he unzips his jeans
the LP pops   I lean back on my elbows
my legs open and bass guitars rumble up through our skin
the music crackles   spirals onto our bodies
points of refracted light snowflaking down   *please please please*
my skates in a tangle on the rink

Joseph makes crazy love to me in time with the music
the violins rise
drums grow louder under the sad
sad lyrics

II.

Last car to pass,
Here I go!

—"Radar Love"

How I Learned to Drive

mom in the driver's seat
of our white '63 Chrysler New Yorker
my brother and sister reading
Archies and love comics in the back
she fishes a lighter and her Cameos
from the huge black purse between us
her other hand leaves the wheel
Drive for a sec
one hand flicks the lighter
the other cups the flame
and I reach across without a thought
an eleven-year-old lost inside
Casino Royale   scarcely lift
my eyes from the page   take the square steering wheel
keep the car straight on the road with one hand
for as many flicks as it takes her lighter to catch
the first whiff of tobacco

she takes the wheel from me
I go back to my book
shoulder line a blur to my right
through an open summer window
on a long prairie highway

Eduardo, My Mustang

the April day mom drives me to pick him up
I sit inside him for hours with the stereo on
his leather driver's seat holds me tight
front disc brakes
staggered rear shocks
Eduardo,
you are my dream car

Gary Numan in the 8-track deck
I play with knobs and clean
cool surfaces   I love how the leather-covered stick
fits inside my palm

saved up my rink money for ages
mom loaned me the rest
he's all mine

my 1974 butterscotch 2-door
Mustang is the most beautiful car in the world
ivory leather interior
my sleek 4-speed Mach I V-6
a leather-wrapped steering wheel
I swear was made for my hands

I turn him on   keep him
in neutral gunning him
till I'm ready to peel out
            oh baby, take me for a ride
start slow on the back roads behind the high school
I turn up my music   shift high into second
rev him screaming till I shift again

we cruise at 80 miles an hour in fourth across
grid road intersections
past farms and ranches
my hair in my face   right hand on the stick
tunes pounding

Power Steering Repair

I take it easy over to Joseph's dad's garage
Eduardo's power steering isn't working right
it's losing fluid and I have to crank it
to make it turn at all

I've had a look at the steering's high-pressure hose
it looks pretty new
but there's a split in the S-curve to the control valve
maybe the hose isn't aligned properly

Joseph leans over my engine
No problem   he says   *We just need to put a support*
under that steel line so it won't vibrate
I'll bet that's what's causing that stress crack

I love it when he talks dirty

I fish through his dad's box of clamps
find a rubber-cushioned one we can attach to the line
without crimping it   I lean in over the side of the motor
hold the clamp in place for him
watch his blackened hands tighten it up
connect the pressure hose to the steering linkage
top up my fluids

That should do it

I pull him to me by the front of his overalls
I knew there was a reason I keep you around
wipe my hands on the curve of his ass
kiss him   breathe him deep
grease and gas and sweet sweet garage

Leaning against the Demon Late on a Friday Night

I fall against Joseph's Demon   he's gunning it
vibrating driver's door reaches right
through me   his window open
he's pumping it   his feet balanced on the pedals
I bend in and give him my tongue

all that smooth green power under me and the stink
of exhaust through cool air
drape myself over the front of the hood
my face on heated metal
hands on fire   legs trembling
"This Flight Tonight" chugging into my veins
I like it dangerous
if he pops the clutch he'll crush me

I can hear air reach through filters   gas spurts into pistons
sparkling   bursting into flame   explode and ferment
my head an oven   horsepower   pistons
slick through fuel and oxygen   gaskets
full with the mix of air and petroleum
my thighs a riot of heat
hips charged and I press
myself against the edge of the hood
the car sings to me
watching Joseph through the windshield
his eyelids go low and loose
one hand high on the wheel

he lets the car settle into neutral
climbs out   I turn to face him
pull his tongue into my mouth
the chugging 440 burning me
my hands hot on the hood
and Joseph rocking me into the thumping grille
one hand at the embroidered back pocket of my jeans
the fabric electric and buzzing
headlights blaze the night either side of our vibrating thighs
his ass pushing me against metal
denim encasing him
my feet up on the bumper and Joseph all over me
do it to me through our clothes
Leave your jeans on   Oh god leave it all on

Slide into My New Ride

I pick him up at the 7-Eleven after work
Joseph slides into my new ride
he smells of long hot shower
transmission fluid and leather
a little sweat and aftershave
he looks nervous
asks why we're not using his car
I need to break mine in
I give him a half-smile and without warning him
I hit the gas   drop the clutch
like he's taught me
a screech of tire out of the lot
not bad for a girl
drag through the industrial park
I rev it high   shift into fourth
take the corner too fast   he grabs the dash

Modern English pounds from my 8-track deck
"I Melt with You"
I pull in behind the rink
pitch black shadows
kill the engine, leave it half-turned so the stereo's still on
lean over the stick   kiss him hard

I'm in the back before he's got his seat belt off
throw my skates to the floor on the driver's side
he slides across leather to the middle
and I straddle him   work him with my thighs
through two pairs of jeans
my Mustang rocks with us

I kick off my suede boots   pull my jeans over a leg
climb back into his unzipped lap and ride
his breathing buried in my hair

I drive him back to the 7-Eleven
I'll cruise around
just for a while   seeping and tired
till mom has gone to bed and I can
sneak back into the house
my car the silent witness

Crazy Love

my skates carry me weightless across the empty floor
they give and squeak in my most graceful side-to-side rexing
the boots hug my ankles
I move to the centre   my arms swing behind me
a speed skater without blades
Poco's gorgeous echoing guitars
brush the bare walls and empty blue
I stop at centre   lift my front wheels
spin easy   balanced on my back wheels
under speakers and lights

there is nothing more than this
my skates   my music   Susan across a Saturday morning rink
Joseph still in bed this early   maybe thinking of me
stroking his memories
a whole hour to ourselves before I have to open
to crowds of birthday parties
rentals and popcorn and the sticky pop hands of little kids

Susan cuts across and grabs my belt loop
her skates match my rhythm
long figure S diagonal to the back corner
I take her hand from my jeans and turn to face her
don't have to tell her   she already knows

Drive the New 1974 Mustang Mach I!

[With optional timing gears, for this year only]

You've blown your timing gears   Joseph tells me
what? timing gears? can't believe I didn't notice that
doesn't it have
chains
belts
like every other car on the fucking planet?

Nope, gears   he says   wiping his hands on a rag
hanging by the door of his dad's garage
my Mustang sits spread wide open
a butterscotch cadaver on a slab of concrete
hood up   bones cracked   pulled wide   liquid heart
leaking on the greasy grey floor
gorgeous parts everywhere
had to tow it here
I don't have the right tools

Well   I sigh   *What am I supposed to do?*
sitting hard on the
steps to his dad's kitchen
I can't replace the gears
I'd have to replace the whole thing
I can't afford that
oh my beautiful car

he takes my shoulders
Yeah, I know   *You have to*
drop in a new transmission

    I wish I knew how to put all this back together
    I know a lot about cars but I don't know
    how to pull gears from the crankshaft

without damaging the engine
the broken parts should come off easy
in my dreams
dreams give you smooth ride and speed
without busted engine parts that can't be repaired

Joseph kisses me   wipes my cheek with an oiled thumb
the scent turns me on
his hands   my face
he unzips his coveralls and I'm in the back seat in a flash
he lifts my waist the way I love it
smudges my collarbone
my car's fluids soaking from his hands into our skin

he drives me home in his Demon
Isn't this car enough for you?
he's joking   trying to make me forget
but I can't laugh   can't cry

Dead Car

my brother Larry asks   can he have the white leather seats
and the rear- and side-view mirrors for his '79 Pinto station wagon
my greasy noisy Mustang small-block parts in a gutless shitbox Pinto

I shudder
Rip out the pieces you want
the heart is gone   might as well donate any viable organs
to save other needy cars
Keith says he wouldn't mind the visors and the headlights
figures they'll both fit his Challenger with a few modifications
says he'll take the wheels too if nobody else wants them
he'll pay me   *Just take them, Keith*

Terry says he could use the wipers and floor mats for his Dart
and I give him the tach assembly too
        it works great
        I watched it hit 8000 rpm just before the timing went
        I panicked   couldn't save my car
        didn't know how to stop it revving
        some things are out of your control
        maybe if I hadn't tried to start it on such a cold day

but damn it, I want that leather-covered steering wheel
the silver Mustang in the centre of the grille
Larry pulls them for me after he's stripped the pistons and the seats
after he's taken the mirrors   the rest of the chrome
I ask him to pull me a head gasket and clean it up
maybe I'll use it as a picture frame
cut out little round photos of me and *Eduardo* in happier times

I hate to look at it sitting there   no tires   no seats
half the motor gone
finally have it towed away
as the truck hoists my baby on the trailer
I toss my new-wave 8-tracks into what was once the front seat

think of it being crushed in one of those machines
that turns a sweet car into a 3-foot-square tangle of metal and glass
fluids squeezed out under pressure staining what leather remains
oozing all over itself in a final mess of liquids and crunching parts

Good Night, Lover

Meet me at the rink after I get off work
We'll have the whole night to skate
but not tonight, Joseph
I have to return Susan's car and
my shift starts in six hours

he holds me against the Nova
kisses delicious soft love into my mouth
his blue eyes a playful, gentle promise

the Demon runs next to us
driver's door open
waiting for the slide of Joseph's hands on its wheel
his thighs against its leather

his hug takes in every inch of me
I bend to him   his strong fingers spread on my back
he takes my lower lip into his mouth

he lets me go   climbs into his car
I'm shaken and warm
the Demon's tires burn   Joseph honks and peels out
his tail lights disappear around the corner of the building
I lay my body against the cool of Susan's car
my face against the roof
let the dark take the burn from my skin

the quiet is complete at this time of night

Snapshots

my car-dreaming tonight is ragged
with black highway thumping exhaust
full of reflections on glass on plastic
in side mirrors and rainslick asphalt Joseph
and me on long black roads into night
church spires roar past
he takes pictures as we drive by
Souvenirs he says
Why I ask *are you going somewhere?*

No

The snapshots won't turn out
I tell him it's night and the car
is driving itself now the wheel makes slight adjustments
on the pitch road
he turns the camera to me in the blue light from the dash
eyes shiny he says
The pictures aren't important
he floats out the passenger side window into night
It's the taking of them that matters

Saturday 1:25 AM

[Corner of Baseline Road and 17th Street]

the reader may want to go downstairs
find Golden Earring's album Moontan
it's in the basement cupboard with the other LPs
a teenage collection that is certainly still there
the reader will recognize it on sight
a golden hoop on a long lobe

pull out the vinyl
hold it by the edges   blow off dust
find "Radar Love"

spin it

turn it up loud

allow the white space to be
punctuated by bass licks and drum solos
let the music be the soundtrack for this poem

Joseph, you'd be nearly home by now
revving high at lights and stop signs
your feet expertly riding the pedals
clutch   and brake   and go!

in my room
I stare the trees' shadows
onto my white walls
reflected night on my roller skates in the corner

"Radar Love" rattles from my stereo
I know you're listening to the same song
our new favourite for speed skate
you   driving away from me

the bass player crawls right inside
this lick   it smokes out of your car

sleepless   sweating   rigid
the singer drives for hours
in the song it's the middle of the night

you're in your '71 Sublime Green 340 GSS
4-Barrel 2-Door Dodge Demon
two hundred and seventy-five horses at 6000 rpm

you stop at the light
Golden Earring spills distorted
from back-window speakers you wired in last week
you turn it up
bass line pounds louder
glass rattles

the thump reaches your groin, your cock twitches
you adjust the mirror   check your gorgeous hair
drum the steering wheel

refinery tanks on the outskirts of Edmonton
stacks pumping filthy in darkness
no other cars around   this light takes
forfuckingever
you rev
the car lurches ahead
            it wants to ride!

the light opposite turns yellow
you smoke your tires   screech out into the intersection

trees etched black on walls
for a long time I don't even blink
light shifts in my room
the bass rumbles through me
pounding drums and screaming vocals
your cock hard   right hand tight on it through jeans

your other hand tight on the wheel

    drunk headlights aim for you
through windshield glass
your left hand on the wheel
the other still in your lap

blinding halogen surge of steel   your ears
deafened at impact   hands pinwheel from the severed
steering column   spine bends in half

metal floats up through cheeks
glass fills your open mouth   your eyes
neck rattles   snaps
the stereo dented but still playing
            shards star the interior
stab upholstery and carpet
your shoulder and neck
speakers hit the side window
a wail of electric guitar bounces inside the shattered car
body smashes through glass over the dashboard
I can see your pelvis   legs
drag over buckled metal
toes scrape jagged glass
my eyes are wide
this drum solo ripping me open

your body slams into the other car
head first against its windshield

side of your skull spiderwebs the glass
leaves a cheek-shaped print
blood at the centre   your tiny golden
earring   a piece of your earlobe lodges
in cracked glass fireworks   exploding gasoline
            wheels spinning
shining against street lights and rain

you slide across his hood   your left arm
broken at the shoulder   scrabbles at wipers

fingers squeak smeared lines
to the edge of the windshield
fingers squeak on the guitar strings
synth and drums speed up and lift
through glass
the band is wild!

the bass line returns

takes its time

holds its own

the reader may want to pause
let these drums fill the lungs and blood vessels

the night is quieter now
hiss of radiator   spin of hubcap into dark
a left arm torn from its socket

your eyes to the stars

leather and denim soaked in chaos
blood and cheap rum   other driver's sour guts rank
refinery smoke
dark hair in breeze

for one moment
you shine against the sky
crazy bleeding fingers on guitars and drumsticks

you spin through the night

smack the pavement

the reader will want to let the song
play out

feel it

to the end

How I Learned to Skate

Susan heard there was a roller rink opening up
you could go in the first weekend
for free   look around without skating
eat a hot dog   take home a helium balloon

we went to the grand opening and tried to look cool
watched the other kids our age
whirling from one end of the rink to the other
their gleaming new skate wheels spinning
this kind of life into our minds

we sat in an orange booth   pretended
not to see the good-looking boys sending
winks and cologne to us
on the artificial breeze
a blond boy with steel blue eyes
loose and free on his skates
tight jeans and a gold chain
his easy grace and complete comfort
on those eight intimidating wheels
where did he learn to skate like that?
blurred bodies in polyester and denim
a twirl of hair
a man's hand at a girl's trim high-waist jeans

I walked past the popcorn at the concession
boys at the foosball table
rolling back and forth one end of the table to the other
I looked stammering at the shining skates for sale
in the Pro Shop next to the rental booth
their pristine white wheels and coloured laces
asked Terry what he thought I should buy

two hundred and fifty dollars with new
All American Dream wheels
Terry loosened the trucks while he fitted me
I owned those skates within an hour

took them home to the big unfinished basement
laced them carefully   lifted myself from the bottom step
my arms out to the sides by instinct

I taught myself to skate forward, backward
cross over and screech to a reverse halt on my toe stops
avoiding the drains where concrete dipped
mom's stocking feet creaking overhead
carrying laundry up shag carpet stairs

technopop on my cheap cassette player
scratchy and distorted
basement transformed into a rink of
purest blue glass   a cloud of graceful teenagers
dancing round one another in a power ballad haze
dazzling wheels, boot covers
disco, perfume, leaning bodies
hugging corners like love

I'm Told You've Died

I know
I saw it   I leave my brother's car
unlocked at the midnight rink
one thin fluorescent in the office
the rest of the empty sprawling room is dark
switch on the small lamp in the DJ booth
till I find the record I want   "Cars" by Gary Numan
lace my skates   turn the song up too loud
take to the floor
speakers distorted   shocked
cracks in the 45 fierce in my trampled brain

I skate   my legs   the breeze   noise
of synthesizers and Gary's thin vocals
my wheels scraping the floor when I slide
to a stop sideways   plastic peeling under
my smoking Dreams
skate hard as I can   blind under a single bulb
heat under the waistband of my jeans
and I slam into the wall punching concrete

a hard skate to the other side of the rink
trip myself deliberately on the low carpeted border
the record is overplayed   it catches and skips

curl up on the blue floor   my lip bleeding
hair across my face and night
outside settles on our cars   mine crushed
yours in pieces
I close my eyes   let my weeping echo the synth-pop
lie inside myself   a needle skipping
its tick and pop matching a muddy hammer in my skull

and you lift me
        dance me to the centre of the rink
            hold me spin me
              hands at my waist a kiss on the cheek
           and I twirl under your hand
      take the waltz position for a diagonal cut to the corner
   in music and disco lights

you lie
under a white sheet   a steaming Demon
towed away   your hand broken where it held mine
Friday nights in the swirl of love   music
spinning perfumed dancers

At the Corner, Night

yeah, so I'm a little drunk
so what? my brother's Pinto is under control
I keep the centre line to my left
doing the speed limit like the sign says

there's no traffic here at three in the morning
I brake hard at the intersection
leave the car idling on the shoulder
driver's door open

on the lamp post
a soggy teddy bear with a silk carnation around its neck
what idiot put that there?
a wet wooden cross
little Jesus in the damp earth
there's a dripping wreath tied to the pole with some twine
and a dozen wilted roses in stiff
plastic wrap

why do people leave this shit?
the dead person doesn't care
Joseph, you weren't religious and you hated
teddy bears
you loved fixing cars   late-night
sex with skating girls and too-loud disco

I tear the roses from the cold metal
inside them is a card from Katie
the writing has run
curled at the edges   *I still love you*
here's a picture of you I've never seen before
you and your Demon at the back of your house

I'm going to take that
tuck it into my back pocket

a roar through the intersection
black Duster full of boys who know they could never
die in that car
they honk at me windblown at the side of the highway
whistle and screech

I wait a long time in the wind
staring at the empty road the Duster's left behind
there's no reason for the light to change
nobody coming from the secondary street
something red glints in the middle of the intersection
that must be right where it happened
roses in my left hand
I steady myself   swallow hard
walk out into the highway
I can hear a truck coming but fuck it
I want that piece of your tail light I can see lying there

a small sideways rain has started
thank god for rain   for how it washes away

through my blurred eyes
my fingers scrape at asphalt
a handful of glass and hard shards of
plastic   gritty road dirt mixed in
the truck driver blows his horn
light changes to yellow   the big rig
screeches to a stop ten feet from me
the teeth of its grille snarled back and howling

reeking exhaust   headlights too bright
the driver yells something out the window
I stand in the road watching sky
the cars collide in my mind
twisted dance of blood and spiral
in dirtyrain nightsky and piercing lights
two moving cars   a splash of metal on glass

I will stand here in slashing night until
my body becomes part of the crash
until I feel punctures
my limbs torn from sockets
street lamps   traffic lights   grisly ballet of arms
legs windshields twirling hubcaps and bouncebounce
of tin on pavement
lit from above by green   yellow   red
blood washed into dirty grass and stone
at the roadside

unsteady stumbling off the pavement
my half crawl and the rig's
thousands of tires rumble bulleting pebbles
past me in sprays of road
water and dirt

I'm wet and on my knees
looking for blood or leather washed here
head bent to the ditch   this is just grass
a piece of orange signal light cutting into my palm

I dig until my hands are empty and raw
and the hole is deep enough
for roses and pieces of your car   fat drops splash
the backs of my hands turning and turning dirt
to mud

I dig   tear petals
from roses in uneven clumps
and line the bottom of the hole
lay the orange and red
remains on top of the petals   cover everything
my knees torn
I lean back face to the sky hands upward
cupped on my lap   kneeling

Funeral

I love a Eurosynth-pop song by Yazoo
about a young man's funeral
how the girlfriend waits till everyone leaves the graveyard
before she says goodbye to her dead boyfriend
        the song won't say how he dies
but I suspect they planned it
        redneck father's shotgun or slashed
        wrists in the tub
        bloodstained note on the tiles
                I decided to leave you now, before I had the chance
                to die.

how they had kissed and wept the night before

to the singer, it seems like everyone
stands around the grave
all the grey day in the rain
dripping raincoats and umbrellas
she is impatient   waiting for them to leave
so she can place her flowers
but by then the writing on her card has run

she sings that she's glad he died
no one had ever understood him
her goth facade running mascara
streaks down her face
the romantic black-cloaked new-wave idea
of death   the ultimate teenage rebellion
take *that*, mindless parents
take *that*, totally fucked world

I don't bring flowers
(what would be the point?)
your friends touch their moist hands and faces
to my cheeks   Susan steers me away
Terry   Katie   your dad   Keith's not here
somebody beat the shit out of him last night
behind the high school

Susan's hands firm on my shoulders
we move to the front of the church
I don't think I can stand on my own
don't know how to do this   I didn't go to the Impala boy's funeral
afraid his parents would blame it all on me
Susan and Terry hold me up at the elbow

I sit in a cold pew   imagine you
maybe thinking of me before your
last moments on Baseline Road
the preacher guy calls me your *Special Friend*

when I get home, I play Gary Numan
loud ("Are 'Friends' Electric?")
I lie alone in my room, the album crackling through my speakers
I know what the chick in that song had written on her card

my bedroom door shut and locked
line my eyes with new-wave black
but it runs as fast as I can put it on
write the note you might have left me
your thoughts of me when you splintered thick glass

in Cars

Susan and I drive all over town in her Nova
they told us *be careful*
so we're not

we zoom past the rink over and over
listening to "Ballroom Blitz"
I'm burning some rubber
you'd have been proud of the smoke I'm making
you always said girls were crap
peeling out
I prove you wrong today
            driving
singing
thinking   how simple everything was last Tuesday
(you were alive
            we made love in the back seat of *Eduardo*
            your *Chick Magnet*)

I was thinking cock
I was thinking love

how could this be okay?
a face I love arcing toward a windshield

what mattered was you and me in cars
you and me steaming through
nights out back of my place
stopping between acreages
dark dark roads   no one to see us
loving each other

no one to see me
open my body to you
we drive in the silent country
your hands and your eyes
a revving 4-Barrel on a deserted
back road
screaming wide open
hear me tell you I wanted your mouth
  your heat
that someday we would have it all
and two cool rides

I hope you didn't know
I want you to have been unconscious
before
you
sparkled the windshield with your life

Facing the Demon

Chick Magnet is out back of your place
your dad hasn't got rid of your car yet
he needs to be with it for a day or two   *closure* he says
but he told me it will be gone
soon   I want to say goodbye

I'm careful and quiet and it's night
your dad's asleep and won't hear me
creak open the back gate and there's your car
cleaned out, unlocked, and waiting to be towed

the driver's door is too smashed
to get in this side
I open the passenger door
it creaks loud   scrapes on itself
the whole frame's shot
and the doors don't open smooth
I stop   hold my breath
watch the upper windows of the house
no lights   I climb in
and pull the door nearly closed

stretch out on the back seat
a breeze inside my open blouse
and it was my fault   you were turned on
distracted and hard when you left me that night
your mouth wet from mine

tomorrow your car will be crushed
into a sharp-edged cube of green metal
and I curl up on the back seat
run my hands on cool leather

the warm heart cold now in death
I should stay back here
feel the tilt and pull of the tow truck
the giant curved claws piercing the hood crashing
through what glass is left in side and rear windows
lifted in swinging equilibrium
to the platform   bits of other cars' tail lights
door handles crushed from their bodies
as the machine presses in
the metal plates approaching from all sides
I want to feel what you felt—
crush of glass in my face
metal thrust through skin

I want to pay for your death
be crushed inside the car's

long

silent

drop

into the pile of dead metal
released by huge steel teeth
a spinning cube falling through air
metallic bounce as bits of glass,
upholstery, flesh crash to earth
—that can be my payment
my heart bursting like yours
dropping through the quiet terror

of destroyed machines
and dead friends

sky just lightening
I stare at the back of the passenger seat
been staring for hours
your car sighs with me   wraps its bulk around my limp arms
it breathes me through night and cold
me watching the shadows of trees against
black leather in moonlight
shadow of branches smoothing my retinas   your car holds me in
holds me together
think nothing   feel nothing
I don't move until your dad reaches in
shakes me a little   gentle
a stab of low sun behind his head
take his hand   he pulls me out

a tow truck idles in the alley
a man with oily hands stands near it
looking at his watch
Susan and Terry sit out front in Terry's Dart
waiting to drive me home

Out behind the 7-Eleven

we cruise past   rev the engine
squeal rubber
teenagers jump in and out of muscle cars
angle-parked at the 7-Eleven
music and smoke bleed from open doors and windows
we pull around back   crunch on gravel
the alley is perfect
I shift into neutral, hit the hand brake
reach over you   open your door

I pull you into the back seat
leather smell and my perfume
fresh vacuumed floor mats
the car is running   pulsing
Billy Idol   "Dancing with Myself"

scrunch of your leather jacket against my jeans
lift your body from the seat
work me closer   open me
move me under you

my muffler chunks under us, coughs sweet
exhaust-spill into the Mustang through open windows
you lean into my body
Billy Idol grunting through my speakers

I can hear the other rink kids
in and out of the squeaky door buying
Slurpees   quenching the post-pot
munchies and I recognize the baby blue '68
'Cuda 340 S next to us

two tongues lacing around one another
hands over a head
a shirt unbuttoned

you're hard between my legs
hands and tongue on me   my breasts
my mouth   I reach to free you and you're
torn from me through the rear window
glass shards tossed into my open blouse
bloodsplash on my boots
spatters my Dreams
you're sucked into the sky arms spread wide
me watching you rise
me in the back seat of my still
-running Mustang

Your Mouth Sweet with Rain

my job is to bring you
back to life
I know how the pieces fit
start with your arm   the least damaged part
I have to move you   roll you
free the broken limb
pop it back into its socket
a deliberate trickle of engine fluids around me
new-made runnels in jagged
cracks of road and skin

I remove your bloody rain-soaked sneakers
set the leg bones
ignore the other driver vomiting out the window
his mouth an O
horn wailing   sound of sirens and rain
the small creaks of suspended traffic
lights swinging in a cross-breeze from town
onlookers stopped by the white light
I've put up around our bodies

your head intact but bleeding
I move to a spot above your hair
my hands at your temples
lids twitch   my warm hands   your broken neck
your eyes on me and I feel you
take the weight of your head from my hands
move it into my lap   I bend to kiss you
your mouth sweet with rain
feel your hips rise from oily pavement
pull me over you
you're ready for me on the road
rain and salt   oil and tears

“Bang a Gong” is the greatest rexing skate song ever
T-Rex and Marc Bolan both gone inside a minute
Marc Bolan dead in a fat, dramatic crash
his Mini GT slammed into a sycamore tree by his girlfriend
she lived   he died   thrown into the back seat
head smashed open   blood mixing with purple
glitter on his eyelids
his grey velour top and pink spandex tights
the Glam Rocker dead in a car on a South London road
a belly full of booze and a two-year-old son at home

this is how it all ends
a ruined car   pieces of guitar   big hair
soaked in blood
a wheel turning   turning on a broken axle
smashed thigh bones inside thrashmetal pants

you stand
guide me to my car and you take the wheel
into night
I watch the street lights above us
the thin yellow falls across my body
each one flashes down the hood

We Ride

you're next to me and we're riding
in my Mustang
all the windows down and winter
pouring in

cold air and swirls of snow
at our faces as I spin out at intersections
on dark back roads and deserted parking lots
speakers pushed to the edge of distortion

I'm driving the way you like it   dangerous
revving to five thousand before I shift
you say you wish every girl
drove like me
you reach over to stroke my thigh
and I settle my leg into your hand
slam the stick into fourth then touch
you with my right hand   your thighs sigh open
shrieking muffler
snow and exhaust a wall behind us

I drive harder   hard as I can
our breath sharp puffs at the dash
light from the fuel gauge and tach
reflect orange in your eyes
the car giving us all it has
thrilled to be under us   letting us ride it harder
we scream past tilted stop signs
an inch thick with snow
my hands leave the wheel
my car takes us and we ride
we ride

Useless Circles

I don't feel like going to the rink
what's the point?
skating around and around in endless useless circles
and for what?
I throw the skates into the back of my closet
the toe stops Joseph bought for me
leave a white smudge when they hit the panelling
laces tangled and worn black from the metal hooks
the boots' mouths

I pull the door shut
they can rot in there

Acknowledgements

deepest love and thanks to my husband Stu for your thoughtful readings of these poems and for all the *Show & Shine* fun.

many thanks to Birk Sproxton—my mentor, guide, and friend—you'd have told me to get on with it, and not allow anything (even the loss of you) to stand in the way of the work.

for many years of editing and friendship, my thanks to the members of my writing groups, formal and informal: Bert Almon, Holly Borgerson Calder, Rebecca Campbell, Olga Costopoulos, Joan Crate, Lee Elliott, Heidi Greco, Leslie Greentree, Catherine Greenwood, Shawna Lemay, Iman Mersal, Blaine Newton, and Michael Penny. J, L, and H: you went above and beyond.

fondest thanks and gratitude to my friends and colleagues, past and present, at Turnstone Press, and especially to Sharon Caseburg who sees my work more clearly than I have ever seen it. heaps of thanks to Dave Elias, Kirsten Koza, and the Olives. to Paula Jane Remlinger: thanks for your kindness and insight at the very early stages. my thanks also to John Weier, Susan Wilson, Rod Schumacher, and Paul Wharton.

thanks to the Alberta Foundation for the Arts, and to the Banff Centre Alberta Artist Short Term Residency Program for writing time. bouquets of wildflowers to Steven Ross Smith and to Mel and Karen at *La Ranchita.* many thanks, as always, to St. Peter's Abbey. thanks to the Saskatchewan Writers Guild Writers/Artists Colonies, 2004 and 2005. thank you, Ken Mansfield, for the beer and the idea.

thank you to B, D, J, S, B, and Wheelies Roller Rink, Sherwood Park, Alberta. I still miss you all. Erindale gang: your love fixed everything. thanks to Larry and Karen for helping me remember, and to Stacey for getting us all back on our skates. I am indebted to Maureen Scott Harris for her lucid explanation of Mudra: the empty bowl. it was exactly what I was trying to write. DC, thank you for becoming my Joseph (albeit unknowingly) and for helping me see him so clearly.

love and thanks to my friends and families: especially Jalesa, Griffin, and Ella.

some of these poems have appeared, in slightly different form, in *Backyard Ashes* (#6), *The Fieldstone Review* (#1), and *Roller Boogie* (*The Olive Chapbook Series*). my thanks to the editors.